I0146332

Edmund Wetmore

Statutory Law of New York Regarding the Insane

Edmund Wetmore

Statutory Law of New York Regarding the Insane

ISBN/EAN: 9783337376352

Printed in Europe, USA, Canada, Australia, Japan

Cover: Foto ©Suzi / pixelio.de

More available books at **www.hansebooks.com**

STATUTORY LAW

OF

NEW YORK

REGARDING THE INSANE.

———•◦•———

By EDMUND WETMORE, Esq.

UTICA, N. Y.
ROBERTS, PRINTER, 60 GENESEE STREET.
1867.

STATUTORY LAW OF NEW YORK REGARD-
ING THE INSANE.*

BY EDMUND WETMORE, ESQ.

I. STATUTORY DISABILITIES OF THE INSANE.

The laws in which the ordinary disabilities of the insane are referred to, are as follows:

1. *Aliening Lands.*—Every person capable of holding lands (except idiots, persons of unsound mind, etc.,) seized, or entitled to any estate or interest in lands, may alien such estate or interest at his pleasure, with the effect and subject to the restrictions and regulations provided by law.

2. *Marriage and Divorce.*—When either one of the parties to a marriage shall be incapable for want of understanding of consenting to a marriage, the marriage shall be void from the time its nullity shall be declared by a court of competent authority.

The Supreme Court may by a sentence of nullity declare void the marriage contract for the cause existing at the time of the marriage that one of the parties was an idiot or lunatic.

3. *Statute of Limitations.*—If a person entitled to commence any action for the recovery of real property, or to make an entry or defence founded on the title to real

---

* This abstract of the principal laws of the State of New York respecting the insane, was compiled some years ago, for the simple purpose of facilitating a comparison between the legislation of our own and our sister States upon that subject. The paper was not intended to be a complete digest even of all our statutes, much less an orderly statement of the law of insanity in New York, as far as settled by legislative enactments and judicial decisions: it merely collates the substance of the statutes referred to, for the convenience of any who desire to know their general and most important provisions.

property, or to rents or services out of the same, be, at the time such title shall first descend or accrue, insane, the time during which such disability shall continue shall not be deemed any portion of the time limited for the commencement of such action, or the making of such entry or defence; but such action may be commenced, or entry or defence made, after the period of twenty years, and within ten years after the disability shall cease, or after the death of the person entitled who shall die under such disability; but such action shall not be commenced, or entry or defence made, after that period.

If a person entitled to bring certain enumerated actions other than actions for the recovery of real property, be, at the time the cause of action accrued, insane, the time of such disability is not part of the time limited for the commencement of the action, except that the period within which the action must be brought cannot be extended more than five years by such disability, nor longer than one year after the disability ceases.

4. *Wills.*—(*a.*) *Real Property.*—All except idiots, persons of unsound mind, married women, and infants, may devise their real estate.

(*b.*) *Personal Property.*—Every male of the age of eighteen, and every female not married of the age of sixteen, of sound mind and memory, and no others, may bequeath personal estate.

II. APPOINTMENT OF COMMITTEES FOR THE INSANE.

[The following proceedings will be found treated of at length in "Creary's Special Proceedings," and the present statement of them is taken mainly from that work.]

1. *Courts which have Jurisdiction.*—In this proceeding the old method, in accordance with the ancient practice of chancery, remains substantially unaltered. The general power of chancery has been transferred to the

Supreme Court, which now supercedes the former Court of Chancery in this State. It is enacted that the Supreme Court shall have the care and custody of all idiots, lunatics, and persons of unsound mind, and of their real and personal estates, so that the same shall not be wasted or destroyed; and shall provide for their safe keeping and maintenance, and for the maintenance of their families and the education of their children, out of their personal estates and the rents and profits of their real estates, respectively. It is also enacted that the County Courts shall have the care and custody of the person and estate of a lunatic, or person of unsound mind, residing within the county, and also such courts shall have jurisdiction with respect to the sale, mortgage or other disposition of the real property of such persons situated within the county.

The same authority is also given to the Court of Common Pleas of the city and county of New York, where the lunatic or person of unsound mind resides in that city, or the property is situated therein. And the like authority is also given to the Superior Court of the city of Buffalo, where the lunatic resides in that city, or the property is situated therein.

In the case of a non-resident lunatic, the Supreme Court may appoint a committee to enable the said committee to obtain control of property in this State. And the court may issue a commission to inquire as to the lunacy of a non-resident, but it cannot be executed beyond the limits of the State. In such case the court will direct it to be issued in such county as may be most convenient.

2. *Who may apply for a Commission.*—There is no restriction: a stranger may apply, though the application of relatives will be entertained in preference, if there is no valid objection to them.

3. *Method of Application.*—The application is based upon a petition to the court of proper jurisdiction, which should be accompanied with affidavits, setting forth the unsound condition of mind of the party, and stating some instances of conduct or language which plainly indicate it. Where the lunatic is a non-resident of the State, the petition must also show that he is the owner of property situated in this State.

4. *The Commission.*—Upon the granting of the petition and entering an order to that effect with the clerk of the court, the commission usually prepared by the attorney for the petitioner will issue. It is usually directed to three persons, commanding them to inquire into the alleged insanity, the time when it began, condition of the alleged lunatic's estate, etc.

5. *Notice that the Commission has issued.*—The party proceeded against as a lunatic is entitled to reasonable notice of the time and place of executing the commission, even though a non-resident. A requisition to this effect is usually inserted in the commission. Dangerous madness, or peculiar circumstances, may excuse this notice.

6. *Place of executing the Commission.*—The order usually directs the commission to be executed at or near the place of residence of the alleged lunatic. Non-residence will dispense with, and other circumstances may modify, however, this provision of the order.

7. *Witnesses.*—Subpœnas may be issued by the commissioners, and the court will enforce them.

8. *Precept for a Jury.*—The commissioners may issue a precept to the sheriff of the county in which the commission is to be executed, commanding him to summon a jury.

9. *Duty of the Sheriff.*—The sheriff will summon not less than twelve nor more than twenty-four jurors. It

is also his duty, if required, to attend the execution of the commission, for the purpose of guarding the jury room, etc.

10. *Proceedings before the Commissioners.*—The party proceeded against is entitled to be present and may have counsel. Before proceeding with the examination the commissioners should require proof of the due service of notice of the execution of the commission. The leading commissioner, usually the first one named in the commission, instructs the jury in the duty assigned them, and administers the oath to them and to the witnesses. The party himself may be inspected and examined. The commissioners, or one of them, after the testimony is closed, should submit the question to the jury in the form of a charge, without arguments of counsel on either side. It is necessary that twelve of the jury should concur in the verdict. The verdict being returned,

11. *The Inquisition is made up accordingly, signed and sealed by the Commissioners and by the Jury.*—The inquisition states the finding of the commission whether the party is a lunatic or not, or any other facts concerning which inquiry was to be made, relative to property, etc.

12. *Return of Commission.*—This is done by annexing the inquisition to the commission, duly indorsing them, and filing them with the clerk of the court.

13. *Proceedings on Return.*—Upon the filing of the return, a motion is made to confirm the finding of the jury. The alleged lunatic or his friends may also apply at the same time for an order to set aside the inquisition, or for leave to traverse it, or for an issue.

14. *Who may be appointed Committee.*—There is no particular restriction as to the person who may be appointed committee. The court will exercise its discre-

tion, and consult the interests of the lunatic. The custody of the person is usually committed to some of the nearest kin.

15. *Appointment of Committee.*—The committee is appointed upon application to the court. The same person may be appointed committee both of the person and of the estate, but where the estate is large it is usual to have a separate committee for each. A reference is frequently directed to ascertain the suitable person to be appointed committee.

16. *Bond of Committee.*—This is required before the committee can enter upon their duties, and must have two sufficient sureties and be approved by a judge of the court. Security may sometimes, however, be dispensed with by the court.

17. *Traverse of Inquisition, etc.*—In England the inquisition may be traversed as a matter of right by the alleged lunatic or his friends. In this State they will order a jury trial to decide the fact, in their discretion. Application for jury trial is founded upon petition, notice to the opposite party, and, usually, affidavits. The inquisition may be set aside for irregularity, or upon proof of an erroneous verdict by the jury in the first instance. •If the lunatic is restored to his reason, application may be made to the court to supercede or suspend the commission, or the commission may be superceded if it has remained unexecuted several years, or for other reasons. So the commission may be superceded for a particular purpose—as, in one instance, to enable the lunatic to make a will, though the case cited is of doubtful authority. If the lunatic be sufficiently recovered to make a will, he is sufficiently recovered to be free from the control of the committee altogether, in most instances. In case of the death or incapacity of the commissioners on the original inquisition, a new one may be directed to be issued.

III. THE DISPOSITION OF THE ESTATES OF LUNATICS, AND THE DUTY OF COMMITTEES.

1. *Duty and authority of the Committee, filing Inventory, &c.*—Every committee of the estate of any idiot, lunatic or person of unsound mind, shall, within six months after their appointment, file in the office of the clerk of the court which appointed such committee, a just and true inventory of the whole real and personal estate of such idiot, lunatic or person of unsound mind, stating the income and profits thereof, and the debts, credits and effects, so far as the same shall have come to the knowledge of such committee. And whenever any property belonging to such estate shall be discovered after the filing of any inventory, it shall be the duty of such committee to file as aforesaid a just and true account of the same from time to time, as the same shall be discovered. Such inventories shall be verified by the oath of the committee, to be taken before a judge of any court of record. The filing of such inventories may be compelled by the order and process usual in such cases, of the court which appointed the committee.

Receivers and committees of lunatics, appointed by any order or decree of the Supreme Court, may sue in their own names for any debt, claim or demand transferred to them or to the possession of which they are entitled as such receiver or committee; and when ordered or authorized to sell such demands the purchaser thereof may sue and recover therefor in his own name, but shall give such security for costs to the defendant as the court in which such suit is brought may direct. In an action prosecuted by a person expressly authorized by statute to sue in his own name, as in the case of the committee of a lunatic, the costs shall be chargeable only upon or collected of the estate, fund or party represented, unless the court shall direct the same to be paid by the plaintiff or defendant personally, for mismanagement or bad faith in such action. A person so expressly authorized by statute may sue without joining with him the person for whose benefit the action is prosecuted.

Under the direction of the court, and subject to the law imposing upon those having the care of lunatics the duty of sending them to the asylum, the entire control of the person of the lunatic rests with the committee, and they are bound to provide for his personal ease and comfort. As a general rule the committee cannot enter into any transaction or contract respecting the property of a lunatic without the authority of the court. If the lunatic's estate is large, and its interests require the employment of an agent or clerk, the court, upon the petition of the committee, will allow him to employ such agent or clerk, and pay him a reasonable compensation for his services out of the income of the estate; but the committee himself can not receive a compensation for services as such clerk beyond his allowance for commissions as the committee.

If waste is committed upon the lands of the lunatic, it is the duty of the committee to apply to the court for an order to restrain it.

Where the lunatic resides in another State and has property in the hands of his committee appointed at the place of his residence, that property is the primary fund for his support, and should be first applied for that purpose by the committee who has control of his person.

2. *Sale, Mortgage or Lease of Lunatic's Real Estate.*— (a.) *For payment of debts.*—Whenever the personal estate of any idiot, lunatic or person of unsound mind, for whom there is a committee appointed, shall not be

sufficient for the discharge of his debts, it shall be the duty of the committee of his estate to apply by petition to the court by which they were appointed, praying for authority to mortgage, lease or sell so much of the real estate of such idiot, lunatic, or person of unsound mind as shall be necessary for the payment of such debts. The said petition shall set forth the particulars and amounts of the estate, real and personal, of such idiot, lunatic or person of unsound mind, the application which may have been made of any personal estate, and an account of the debts and demands existing against such estate.

On the presenting of such petition, it shall be referred to a referee, or to the clerk of the court, to inquire into and report upon the matters therein contained, whose duty it shall be to examine into the truth of the representations made, to hear all parties interested in such real estate, and to report thereon with all convenient speed.

If, upon the coming in of the report and an examination of the matter, it shall appear to the court that the personal estate of the idiot, lunatic, or person of unsound mind is not sufficient for the payment of his debts, and that the same has been applied to that purpose, as far as the circumstances of the case rendered proper, an order shall be entered, directing the mortgage, leasing or sale of the whole or such part of the said real estate as shall be necessary to discharge the said debts.

The court may require any additional security to be given by any such committee, for the faithful application and accounting for the proceeds of such mortgage, lease or sale; and may require an account thereof to be rendered from time to time.

In the application of any moneys raised by any such mortgage, lease or sale, the committee shall pay all debts in an equal proportion, without giving any preference to such as are founded on sealed instruments.

(*b.*) *For Support.*—When the personal property and the rents, profits, and income of the real estate of any such idiot, lunatic, or person of unsound mind shall be insufficient for his maintenance, or that of his family, or for the education of his children, a similar application may be made by the committee to the Supreme Court, or to the court having jurisdiction, for authority to mortgage or sell the whole or so much of the real estate as shall be necessary for that purpose; upon which the same reference and proceedings shall be had, a like order shall be entered, as hereinbefore directed in the case of the application for a sale, mortgage, or lease in order to pay the debts of such insane person.

In the case last mentioned, the court shall direct the manner in which the proceeds of such sale shall be secured, and the income or produce thereof appropriated.

The court shall give such orders respecting the time and manner of any sale herein mentioned as shall be deemed proper; and no conveyance in pursuance of any such sale shall be executed until the sale shall have been reported on the oath of the committee, and confirmed by the court directing the same.

(*c.*) *Sale where the Interest of the Lunatic will be Promoted.*—By a late statute, a lunatic may by committee, or by the husband if the lunatic is a married woman, apply to the Supreme Court for the sale of any estate or interest in lands belonging to such lunatic. On such application the said committee, or the said husband, shall give bond to the lunatic (in addition to the bond given on the appointment of such committee,) to be filed with the clerk of the court, in such penalties and with such sureties as the court shall direct, for faithful performance of the trust imposed, accounting for all moneys received, and obeying all orders and directions of the court in relation to the trust, which bond if forfeited shall be prosecuted, by direction of the court, for the benefit of the party injured. Upon the filing of the bond the court may proceed in a summary manner, by reference, to inquire into the merits of the application, and whenever it shall appear satisfactory that the disposition of any part of the real estate or interest in lands of such lunatic, including the separate estate of any married woman who may be a lunatic, is necessary and proper either for the support and maintenance of such lunatic or for his education, or that the interest of such lunatic requires or will be substantially promoted by such disposition, on account of any part of such property being exposed to waste and dilapidation, or on account of its being wholly unproductive, or when the same has been contracted to be sold and a conveyance thereof cannot be made by reason of such lunacy, or for any other peculiar reasons or circumstances, the court may order the letting for a term of years, or the sale or other disposition of such real estate or interest, to be made by such committee in such manner and with such restrictions as shall be deemed expedient, or may order the fulfillment of said contract by conveyance by such committee according to the terms of the contract but no such real estate or interest shall be sold, leased, or disposed of in any manner against the provisions of any last will or of any conveyance by which such estate, or term, or interest was devised or granted to such lunatic.

The agreement to sell, etc., must be reported to the court as in other cases, and if the report be confirmed a conveyance will be executed under the directions of the court.

All sales, etc., made in good faith by such committee, in pursuance of such orders, shall be valid and effectual as if made by such lunatic when of sound mind.

The disposition of the proceeds of the property sold, etc., shall be made according to the order of the court, so as to secure the same for the benefit of such lunatic; and shall require accounts to be rendered periodically by any committee or other person who may be intrusted with the income of such proceeds. No sale, made in the manner provided, shall have the effect of giving the lunatic any other or greater interest or estate in the proceeds of the sale than he had in the estate sold, but the proceeds shall be deemed real estate of the same nature as the property sold. Acceptance of a gross sum may be granted in lieu of dower when a dower interest is the subject of sale, where the person entitled thereto shall consent in writing, or may direct the securing of a reasonable annuity in lieu of dower. But before any such sum shall be paid, or such annuity secured, the court shall be satisfied that an effectual release of such right of dower has been executed.

3. *Application for Conveyance where the Lunatic is Trustee, Specific Performance of his Agreements, Partition of his Estate, &c.*—Whenever any such idiot, lunatic, or person of unsound mind shall be seized or possessed of any real estate by way of mortgage, or as trustee for others in any manner, his committee may apply to the Supreme Court for authority to convey and assure such real estate to any other person or persons entitled to such conveyance or assurance, in such manner as the said court shall direct; upon which a reference and the like proceedings shall be had as in the case of an application to sell real estate, as before

mentioned; and the court, upon hearing all the parties interested, may order such conveyance or assurance to be made.

On the application of any person entitled to such conveyance or assurance, by bill or petition, the committee may be compelled by the Supreme Court, on a hearing of all parties interested, to execute such conveyance or assurance.

Every conveyance, mortgage, lease and assurance, made under the order of the Supreme Court, or of any court having jurisdiction, shall be as valid and effectual as if the same had been executed by such idiot, lunatic, or person of unsound mind when of sound memory and understanding.

The Supreme Court shall have authority to decree and compel the specific performance of any bargain, contract or agreement which may have been made by any lunatic, idiot, or person of unsound mind while such lunatic or other person was capable to contract; and to direct the committee of such person to do and execute all necessary conveyances and acts for that purpose.

The real estate of any idiot, lunatic or person of unsound mind shall not be leased for more than five years, or mortgaged or aliened or disposed of otherwise than as above directed.

In case any lunatic or other such person shall be restored to his right mind, his real and personal estate shall be restored to him.

In case of the death of any idiot, lunatic or person of unsound mind, the power of any trustees appointed as above shall cease, and his real estate shall descend to his heirs, and his personal estate be distributed among his next of kin, in the same manner as if he had been of sound mind and memory; but nothing in the foregoing provisions contained shall be held to affect the provisions of any last will and testament duly made, and which shall be duly admitted to probate.

4. *Effect of Issuing Commission, and of Inquisition.*— After a commission has been issued, persons purchasing property of, or otherwise dealing with the alleged lunatic, with a knowledge that the same has been issued, will do so at the risk of having their whole proceedings declared illegal and void.

The acts of a lunatic before he has been judicially declared to be of unsound mind are not void, but voidable. The courts of this State will not interfere to exonerate a lunatic from liability on his contract for property sold to him, if he has actually had the benefit of the property, and the contract was made in good faith, without knowledge of the incapacity, and where no advantage has been taken of the situation of the party. But, after his incapacity has been judicially ascertained, he can, as before stated, make no contract, nor delegate any power, nor waive any right, until his restoration to capacity is, in like manner, judicially declared.

With respect to acts done by a lunatic before the issuing of a commission, and which are over-reached by the finding of the jury on the commission, that is, where the jury by their return find that the lunatic was insane at the time of the acts in question, the inquisition is presumptive but not conclusive evidence of their invalidity.

IV. LEGAL PROCEEDINGS IN WHICH LUNATICS ARE PARTIES, AND THE SERVICE OF LEGAL PROCESS UPON THEM.

1. *Actions by or against an Insane Person for whom a Committee has been appointed.*—(*a.*) *By such person.*— Receivers and committees of lunatics, appointed by any order of the court, may sue in their own names for any debt to the possession or control of which they are entitled; and, when ordered or authorized to sell such de-

mands, the purchaser may sue and recover therefor in his own name, but shall give such security for costs as the court may direct.

Other actions affecting the person or property of the lunatic, except those above enumerated, must, by common law, be brought in the name of the lunatic, and not in the name of his committee. The New York Code has still further enlarged the power of the committee to sue. It is enacted that a trustee of an express trust, or a person expressly authorized by statute, may sue without joining with him the person for whose benefit the action is prosecuted, and that " a trustee of an express trust," shall be construed to mean a person with whom, or in whose name, a contract is made for the benefit of another. It has been held that the committee of an insane person is the trustee of an express trust, within the meaning of this section.

(*b.*) *Actions against such Persons.—Leave to sue.*— After a person is declared by inquisition to be insane, it is a contempt of court for a creditor, or other person, who is informed of the proceedings to sue the insane person, or levy an execution on his property, or otherwise interfere with it, without the leave of the court. And such creditor or other person, upon a proper application from the committee, will be restrained from such interference.

The proper course for the creditor, under such circumstances, when his claim is disputed or refused by the committee, is to apply to the court, by petition, for the payment of his debt out of the insane person's estate ; or for leave to collect his claim by action, or to have a reference. If the court is satisfied that the debt is justly due, it will order the committee to pay it out of the estate ; or, if doubtful, order a reference, or permit the party to establish his claim by action, in their discretion.

2

• *Mode of Conducting the Action. In general the action should be against the insane person alone.*—In a case in which the committee has a personal interest in the controversy which may conflict with the insane person's, both should be made parties, and the court will appoint a guardian *ad litem* for the insane person.

Service of the Summons.—A civil action is commenced by the service of a summons. If the action be against a person judicially declared to be of unsound mind, and for whom a committee has been appointed, the summons may be served by delivering a copy thereof to such committee and to the defendant personally.

Provisional Remedies in an Action.—An insane person for whom a committee has been appointed, is not, of course, liable to arrest.

Effect of Judgment.—The judgment will bind the estate of the lunatic, and, as has already been seen, the committee may be compelled to perform his contract.

2. *Actions by or Against an Insane Person for whom no Committee has been appointed.* (*a.*) *Actions by such person.*—Until a person is judicially declared to be of unsound mind, there is nothing to prevent the commencement of an action in his own name. The proper course in such a case would be for the opposite party to apply to the court to have a committee appointed in the usual way.

(*b.*) *Actions against such Persons.*—A civil action may be carried on against an insane person, etc., in the same manner as against a sane person, the process being personally served. The insanity of the party defendant, however, would be good ground for opening a judgment rendered against him.

Provisional Remedies in such Action.—If any person imprisoned on attachment, or any civil process, be-

comes insane, the county judge of the county where
he is confined shall institute a careful investigation,
call two respectable physicians and other credible witnesses, and if necessary call a jury, notice of the proceedings having been first given by mail or otherwise
to the plaintiff or his attorney, if in the State; and if
it shall be proved to the satisfaction of said judge that
the prisoner is insane, he may discharge him from imprisonment, and order him into safe custody, and to be
sent to the asylum. Nevertheless, the creditor may
renew his process, and arrest again his debtor when of
sound mind.   *

3. *Other Legal Proceedings.*—In special proceedings,
such for instance as summary proceedings before justices of the peace, for the ejectment of tenants, the
insanity of the party proceeded against would not be
a defence. The proceeding would be conducted as
usual, the committee, if there was one, being made a
party.

Legal papers and process affecting an insane person
must be served upon the insane person personally, if no
committee has been appointed. If a committee has
been appointed it should be served upon both, in
most instances. In some cases, service upon the committee alone would be sufficient.

Sometimes a petition or affidavit is sworn to by one
who has been found by an inquisition to be of unsound mind. In such a case the officer before whom it
is sworn should state in the jurat that he had examined
the petitioner or deponent for the purpose of ascertaining
the state of his mind, and whether he was capable of
understanding the nature and object of the petition or
affidavit, and that he was apparently of sound mind,
and capable of understanding the same. And if the
party is blind the officer should also certify that the

petition or affidavit was carefully and correctly read over to him, in the presence of such officer, before it was sworn to.

V. LAWS REGARDING THE ADMISSION OF THE INSANE TO ASYLUMS, AND THEIR DISCHARGE THEREFROM.

1. *Persons Furiously Mad.*—(*a.*) *Who may commit such Persons to custody.*—When any person, by lunacy or otherwise, becomes furiously mad, or so far disordered in his senses as to endanger his own person or the person or property of others if permitted to go at large, and who is possessed of sufficient property to maintain himself, it shall be the duty of the committee of his person and estate to send him to the State Lunatic Asylum, or to such public or private asylum as may be approved by a standing order or resolution of the supervisors of the county.

If such person is not possessed of sufficient property to maintain himself, it shall be the duty of the father and mother and the children of such person, being of sufficient ability, to send him to the State Asylum or to a public or private asylum, as above mentioned.

In case of the refusal or neglect of any committee of such lunatic or mad person, or of his relatives, to send such person to the asylum, as aforesaid, or when there is no such committee or relative of sufficient ability, it shall be the duty of the overseers of the poor of the city or town where any lunatic or mad person shall be found, to apply to any two justices of the peace of the same city or town, who, upon being satisfied upon examination that it would be dangerous to permit such lunatic to go at large, shall issue their warrant, directed to the constables and overseers of the poor of such city or town, commanding them to cause such lunatic or mad person to be apprehended, and to be safely locked up and confined in such secure place as may be provided by the overseers of the poor to whom the same shall be directed, within the town or city of which such overseers may be officers, or within the county in which such city or town may be situated, or in the county poor-house in those counties where such houses are established, or in such private or public asylum as may be approved by any standing order or resolution of the supervisors of the county in which such city or town may be situated, or in the Lunatic Asylum of the city of New York; but such lunatic or mad person shall not be so confined for longer than the space of ten days, but within that time shall be sent to the said State public or private asylum, as before mentioned.

Any two justices of the peace of the city or town where any such lunatic or mad person may be found, may, without the application of any overseers of the poor, and upon their own view or upon the information or oath of others, whenever they deem it necessary, issue their warrant for the apprehension and confinement of such lunatic or mad person, for not longer than ten days, as aforesaid, and such lunatic or mad person shall in like manner be sent to the said State or private asylum.

In all the above cases it is provided that the lunatic shall be sent to the asylum within ten days. Temporary confinement in other places, not exceeding ten days, may be allowed. No such insane person, however, can be so temporarily confined in any prison, jail or house of correction, unless an agreement shall have been made for that purpose with the keepers thereof, nor shall such person be confined in the same room with any person charged with or convicted of any crime.

(*b.*) *How the duty of committing such Persons to custody may be enforced, and the mode of such commitment.*—The overseers of the poor shall have the same remedies to compel relatives of insane persons, being of sufficient ability, to fulfill the requirements of the provisions above recited, and to collect the costs and charges of non-fulfillment as are given by law in the case of poor and impotent persons becoming chargeable to any town, and it shall be the duty of the overseers of the poor to whom a justice's warrant shall be directed, as above provided, to procure a suitable place for the temporary confinement of such lunatic, as therein directed.

An overseer of the poor, constable, keeper of a jail, or other person, who shall confine any lunatic or mad person in any other manner or in any other place than such as are by law prescribed, shall be deemed guilty of a misdemeanor, and on conviction shall be liable to a fine not exceeding two hundred and fifty dollars, or to imprisonment not exceeding one year, or to both, in the discretion of the court before which the conviction shall be had.

The county superintendents of the poor shall have all the powers and authority above given to overseers of the poor of any town, and both superintendents and overseers are severally enjoined to see that the provisions of law regarding the transfer of the.insane to the asylum be carried into effect in the most humane and speedy manner, as well in case the lunatic or his relatives are of sufficient ability to defray the expenses as in case of a pauper.

In every case of confinement of a lunatic or mad person, as herein above mentioned, (in the asylum or elsewhere,) whether of a pauper or not, neither justices, superintendents or overseers of the poor shall order or approve of such confinement without having the evidence of two reputable physicians under oath as to the alleged fact of insanity, and such testimony shall be reduced to writing, and filed, with a brief report of all the other proofs, facts and proceedings in the case, in the office of the county clerk; and said clerk shall file said papers and register, with dates, the names and residence of the lunatic and officers, severally, in tabular form, in the book of miscellaneous records kept in said office, and the certificate of said clerk, and seal of the court, verifying such facts, shall warrant such lunatic's admission into the asylum.

If any lunatic confined under the laws herein before mentioned, or any friend in his behalf, be dissatisfied with any final decision or order of the justices, or of any overseer or superintendent of the poor under such laws, he may, within three days after such order or decision, appeal to one of the judges of the county, making complaint on oath, and such judge shall thereupon stay his being sent out of the county, and forthwith call a jury to decide upon the fact of lunacy; after a full and fair investigation, aided by the testimony of two respectable physicians, if such jury shall find him sane the judge shall forthwith discharge him, otherwise he shall confirm the order for his being immediately sent to an asylum. In case the justices refuse to make an order for confinement, they shall state their reasons for such refusal in writing, so that any person aggrieved thereby may appeal as above to a county judge, who shall hear and determine the matter in a summary way or call a jury, as he may think most fit and proper. In every case of appeal the judge shall have the same power to take testimony and compel the attendance of witnesses and jurors as a justice has in civil cases.

2. *Indigent Persons, not Paupers.*—When a person in indigent circumstances, not a pauper, becomes insane, application for a certificate of admission to the asylum may be made in his behalf to the county judge of the

county where he resides; but no such certificate can be granted unless the person has become insane within one year next prior to the granting of the certificate by the judge. It is the duty of the judge, when such an application is made to him, to cause such notice thereof, and of the time and place of hearing the same, to be given to one of the superintendents of the poor of the county chargeable with the expense of supporting such person in the asylum, if admitted, or, if such expense is chargeable to a town or city, then to an overseer of the poor of such town or city, as he may deem reasonable. The judge, at the time and place of hearing, must call two respectable physicians and other credible witnesses, and fully investigate the facts of the case, and (either with or without the verdict of a jury, at his discretion, as to the question of insanity,) must decide the case as to his indigence. He must also enquire as to the time when the person became insane. He has power to compel the attendance of witnesses and jurors. Upon all the facts being proven, according to law, it is the duty of the judge to make and execute a certificate that satisfactory proof has been adduced showing the person to be insane, and that he became insane within one year next prior to the date of the certificate, and that his estate is insufficient to support him and his family, (or, if he has no family, himself,) under the visitation of insanity.

The certificate must be authenticated by the county clerk, under his hand and the seal of the county court, and when authenticated is authority for carrying such insane person to the asylum, and must be taken by the friend having such person in charge, and delivered to the superintendent of the asylum. Such person is then to be admitted, and supported at the expense of the county until restored to soundness of mind, if effected in two years.

It is the duty of the judge to file the certificate of the physician called before him, taken under oath, and other papers, with a report of his proceedings and decisions, with the clerk of the county, and also to report the facts of the case to the supervisors, whose duty it is, at their next annual meeting, to raise the money requisite to meet the expenses of support accordingly.

When an indigent patient, under a judge's certificate, has remained in the asylum two years and has not recovered, it is the duty of the superintendent to send notice thereof, by mail, to the overseer of the poor of the town from which the patient was sent, or to the county judge, stating that he should be removed from the asylum, and that if he is not removed his expenses will be chargeable to the county until the removal is made; but in every case of an indigent patient who has remained in the asylum two years and not recovered, the managers may, in their discretion, return him to the county from which he came, and charge the expense of the removal to the county.

When an insane person, in indigent circumstances, shall have been sent to the asylum by his friends, who have paid his bills therein for six months, if the superintendent shall certify that he is a fit patient, and likely to be benefited by remaining in the institution, the supervisors of the county of his residence are authorized and required, upon an application under oath in his behalf, to raise a sum of money sufficient to defray the expenses of his remaining there another year, and pay the same to the treasurer of the asylum; and they shall repeat the same for two succeeding years, upon like application, and the production of a new certificate each year of like import from the superintendent.

The county judge of each of the counties of this State is hereby authorized to send all such indigent lunatics belonging to each county as may be brought before him, either to the county poor-house or to the State Lunatic Asylum, as in his judgment may be for the best interests of all concerned.

Whenever a county judge shall be precluded from acting in the proceedings above mentioned by reason of relationship by consanguinity or affinity to any lunatic in indigent circumstances, application may be made in behalf of such lunatic to one of the justices of the sessions resident of the county in which such lunatic resides, and the same proceedings had before such justices as might be had before the county judge, but for the latter's disability.

3. *Criminals, and Persons under Criminal Charge, and Persons in Prison, &c.*—When a person shall have escaped indictments, or shall have been acquitted of a criminal charge upon trial, on the ground of insanity, the court, being certified by the jury, or otherwise, of the fact, shall carefully inquire and ascertain whether his insanity, in any degree, continues; and if it does shall order him in safe custody, and to be sent to the asylum.

If any person in confinement under indictment, or under sentence of imprisonment, or under a criminal charge, or for want of bail for good behavior, or for keeping the peace, or for appearing as a witness, or in consequence of any summary conviction, or by order of any justice, or under any other than civil process, shall appear to be insane, the county judge of the county where he is confined shall institute a careful investigation, call two respectable physicians and other credible witnesses, invite the district attorney to aid in the investigation, and, if he deem it necessary, call a jury, (and for that purpose is fully empowered to compel the attendance of witnesses and jurors,) and if it be satisfactorily proved that he is insane may discharge him from imprisonment and order his safe custody and removal to the asylum, where he shall remain until restored to his right mind; and then, if the said judge shall have so directed, the superintendent shall inform the said judge and the county clerk and the district attorney thereof, so that the person so confined may, within sixty days thereafter, be remanded to prison and criminal proceedings be resumed, or otherwise discharged; or if the period of his imprisonment shall have expired, he shall be discharged.

If, as already stated, a person imprisoned on attachment or any civil process, or for non-payment of a militia fine, becomes insane, the county judge shall institute like proceedings as are provided for in the last-mentioned case ; but notice shall, in such case, be given by mail or otherwise to the plaintiff or his attorney, if in the State ; and if it shall be proven to the satisfaction of said judge that the prisoner is insane, he may discharge him from imprisonment, and order him into safe custody, and to be sent to the asylum. Nevertheless the creditor may renew his process, and arrest again his debtor when of sound mind.

Persons charged with misdemeanors and acquitted on the ground of insanity, may be kept in custody and sent to the asylum in the same way as persons charged with crime.

4. *Idiots, Paupers, and other Insane Persons not included in the previous classes.*—The county superintendents of any county, and the overseers of the poor of any town, to which any person shall be chargeable who shall be or who shall become a lunatic, *are required* to send such lunatic within ten days to the State Lunatic Asylum, or to such public or private asylum as shall be approved by a standing order or resolution of the superintendents of the county.

It is made the duty of superintendents and overseers (as before mentioned,) to see that the provisions of law in reference to sending the insane to the asylum, be carried into effect in the most humane and speedy manner.

Idiots.—There shall be received and supported gratuitously in the State Asylum for Idiots one hundred and twenty pupils, to be selected in equal numbers, as near as may be, from each judicial district, from those whose parents or guardians are unable to provide for their support, therein to be designated as State pupils; and such additional number of idiots as can be conveniently accommodated may be received into the asylum by the trustees, on such terms as may be just. But no idiot shall be received into the asylum without there shall have been first lodged with the superintendent thereof a request to that effect, under the hand of the person by whose direction he is sent, stating the age and place of nativity, if known, of the idiot, his christian and surname, the town or city and county in which they severally reside, the ability or otherwise of the idiot, his parents or guardians to provide for his support in whole or in part, and if in part only then what part, and the degree of relationship or other circumstance of connection between him and the person requesting his admission; which statement shall be verified in writing by the oath of two disinterested persons, residents of the same county with the idiot, acquainted with the facts and circumstances so stated, and certified to be credible by the county judge of the same county; and no idiot shall be received into said asylum unless the county judge of the county liable for his support shall certify that such idiot is an eligible and proper candidate for admission to said asylum, as aforesaid.

Discharge of Patients from the State Asylum.—The managers, upon the superintendent's certificate of complete recovery, may discharge *any patient*, except one under a criminal charge, or liable to be remanded to prison. And they may discharge any patient admitted as dangerous, or any patient sent to the asylum by the superintendents or overseers of the poor, or by a county judge, upon the superintendent's certificate that he or she is harmless, and will probably continue so, and is not likely to be improved by further treatment in the asylum,—or, when the asylum is full, upon a like certificate that he or she is manifestly incurable, and probably can be rendered comfortable at the poor-house; so that preference may be given, in the admission of patients, to recent cases of insanity of not over one year's duration.

The managers may discharge and deliver any patient, except one under criminal charge, as aforesaid, to his relatives or friends who will undertake with good and approved sureties for his peaceable behavior, safe custody and comfortable maintenance, without further public charge. *A patient of the criminal class* may be discharged by order of one of the justices of the Supreme Court, if upon due investigation it shall appear safe, legal and right to make such order.

The whole duty of the discharge and removal of patients (except in criminal cases,) is devolved upon the managers and the superintendent of the asylum. The county judges, justices, superintendents and overseers of the poor have no authority to discharge or remove them. When a discharge is desired, application must be made to the superintendent, so that it may be considered.

The managers are, by a late law, authorized to appoint two or more of the attendants and employees of the asylum as policemen, whose duty it shall be, under the orders of the superintendent, to arrest and return to the asylum insane persons who may escape therefrom.

Discharge of patients from County poor-houses, etc.— No insane person confined in any county poor-house or county asylum shall be discharged therefrom by any keeper of such establisment, by any superintendent of the poor, or by any other county authority, without an order from a county judge or judge of the Supreme Court, founded upon satisfactory evidence that it is "safe, legal and right" to make such discharge, as regards the individual and the public. The violation of this provision shall be deemed a misdemeanor, and be punishable by a fine not exceeding five hundred dollars nor less than one hundred dollars, in the discretion of the court.

VI. LAWS REGARDING INSANE CONVICTS.

1. *Admission into State Asylum for Insane Convicts.*— Whenever the physician of either of the state prisons of this State shall certify to the board of inspectors or to the inspector in charge that any convict confined therein is insane, it shall be the duty of such board or of such inspector in charge to make immediately a full examination into the condition of such convict, and if satisfied that he is insane the said board of inspectors or the inspector in charge may order the agent or warden of the prison where such convict is confined forthwith to convey said convict to the State Asylum for Insane Convicts, at Auburn, and to deliver him to the superintendent thereof, who is hereby required to receive him into the said asylum and retain him there until legally discharged.

Whenever any convict in the State Asylum for Insane Convicts shall continue to be insane at the expiration of the term for which he was sentenced, the board of inspectors, upon the superintendent's certificate that he is harmless and will probably continue so, and that he is not likely to be improved by farther treatment in the asylum, or upon a like certificate that he is manifestly incurable and can probably be rendered comfortable at the county alms-house, may cause such insane convict to be removed, at the expense of the State, from said asylum to the county wherein he was convicted, or to the county of his former residence, and delivered to and placed under the care of the superintendent of the poor of such county, and the said superintendent is hereby required to receive such insane convict under his charge; they may also discharge and deliver any convict whose sentence has expired, and who is still insane, to his relatives or friends who will undertake, with good sureties, to be approved by said superintendent of the State Asylum for Insane Convicts, for his peaceable behavior, safe custody and comfortable maintenance without further public charge; and no convict shall be retained in the said State Asylum for Insane Convicts after the expiration of his sentence to the state prison, unless by the order of the county judge of the county in which said asylum is situated; and the said county judge, upon the application of the said superintendent, shall proceed to investigate the question of the insanity of such convict, and shall cause two respectable physicians to be designated by him to examine said convict, and upon their evidence under oath, and upon such other testimony as he shall require, shall decide the case as to his insanity, and if he is satisfied that such convict is insane shall make an order that the said convict shall be retained in the said asylum until he is recovered of his insanity, or is otherwise discharged according to law.

2. *Discharge of Insane Convicts from the Asylum.*— Whenever any convict who shall have been confined in

the said asylum as a lunatic shall have become restored to reason, and the medical superintendent of said asylum shall so certify in writing, he shall be forthwith transferred to the Auburn State Prison, and the agent and warden of said prison shall receive said convict into the said prison, and shall in all respects treat such convict as if he had been originally sentenced to imprisonment in said prison, though said convict may have been conveyed to the said asylum from either of the other prisons of this State.

RECAPITULATION OF THE FOREGOING LAWS.

1. *Disabilities of the Insane.*—The incapacity of the insane to perform any legal act is a familiar part of the law of all the United States, as well as of all civilized countries.

The only questions of difficulty arise in the application of this principle to actual cases, when it becomes necessary to define the degree of insanity which amounts to legal incapacity, particularly in regard to criminal responsibility, or the power to make a will. The rules established in New York upon these points are only to be gathered from the reports, and constitute no part of our statutory law.

2. *Custody of the Person and Estate of the Insane.*— The general care of the insane is committed to the Supreme Court. To that tribunal application must be had to obtain the appointment of a committee, and the question of the insanity of the alleged lunatic is decided by a jury. Upon the recovery of the insane person for whom a committee has been appointed he is himself at liberty to apply to the court, and the question whether the commission should be superseded will be judiciously investigated.

The policy of the statute, which substantially follows the common law and exhibits the same jealous regard for personal liberty, is to throw the protection of a jury trial and open judicial investigation around every case of alleged insanity, and to prevent, as far as possible, the deprivation of liberty or the control of property without ample proof of the necessity of such deprivation, and to supply ready means to obtain both liberty and property when the necessity for restraint no longer exists.

Those who are intrusted with the property of the insane stand on the same footing with other guardians, and by heavy bonds and severe penalties are held to the faithful performance of their trust; abuses undoubtedly occur from the occasional dishonesty of committees, just as others acting in a fiduciary capacity sometimes take advantage of their position, and are not detected, but the fault lies not in the law itself but in the neglect, ignorance or corruption of those who administer it.

3. *Legal Proceedings Affecting the Insane.*—There is no difficulty in conducting legal proceedings for or against the insane when a committee has been appointed, and in case such proceedings become necessary, the proper course is to immediately apply for the appointment of a committee. Otherwise, although the course of proceeding will be the same as in case of a person of sound mind and memory, a judgment obtained or other judicial determination made will be liable to be set aside at the instance of the insane person, upon his recovery. It will be seen, however, that there is no adequate protection afforded to an insane person in the possession of property, for whom no committee has been appointed, against designing relatives or others who might enforce fraudulent claims against the property of such an one, and inflict an injury which could never be remedied. It would be well if there was a

statute requiring all legal process sought to be served upon a patient at an asylum to be submitted to the superintending physician, and to make it the duty of the latter to report the fact to the court where the proceedings have been instituted. It will be seen that in some instances personal service upon the insane person is proper, as part of a formal proceeding, but the mode suggested would give immediate information to the court of any attempt to make an improper use of the forms of law.

The only protection against the imprisonment of the insane on civil process is the power given to the county judge to discharge one so imprisoned, and send him to the asylum.

4. *Admission to and Discharge from Asylums.*— When a person becomes violently insane, so as to endanger the security of himself or of others, the duty of sending him to the asylum is compulsory, and may be enforced by legal proceedings. This duty, it will be seen, devolves upon various parties in succession, first upon the relatives, and then upon the public officers of the town or county where such insane person resides. So criminals, or persons under criminal charge, or persons in prison, if insane and their insanity satisfactorily established by the mode directed in the statute, not only may but must be sent to the asylum; and the omission to do so is a breach of duty upon the part of the county judge within whose jurisdiction the case arises. The proper county or town officers, also, are required to send to the asylum those insane persons who would otherwise become a public burden.

In the case of all other insane persons, it is left to their own option, or the option of those having them in charge, whether or not they will send them to the asylum. Certain provisions are made for indigent persons not paupers, and idiots are provided for at the State Asylum for Idiots, at Syracuse.

As has already been said, the whole duty of discharging patients, other than criminals, depends upon the managers and superintendent of the asylum. In case of a wrongful detention by these officers, the remedy would be an action of false imprisonment.

5. *Insane Convicts.*—The duty of sending insane convicts to the asylum for such persons devolves primarily upon the physician of the prison, whose duty it is to certify to the insanity of the convict. There is an old statute which allows the warden or inspector to institute an investigation into the sanity of any convict; and in event the physician should neglect to perform his duty, it is possible the statute referred to would enable the warden to remedy the neglect. The point, however, has never been decided.

www.ingramcontent.com/pod-product-compliance
Lightning Source LLC
Chambersburg PA
CBHW021452090426
42739CB00009B/1735

* 9 7 8 3 3 3 7 3 7 6 3 5 2 *